I0422873

THE FREEDOM TO BE

THE ANGRY
BLACK WOMAN

LISA FRITSCH

Introduction

Harriet Tubman
Abolitionist, revolutionist, humanitarian and escaped slave. Founder of The Underground Railroad. Angry Black Woman.

My daughter Elenor is an exceptional and enthusiastic student. She works hard, a lot harder than anyone might guess to exceed expectations and doesn't take her grades and accomplishments for granted. We've followed the thinking of congratulating her hard work rather than praising her smarts so that she understands the value of effort. Her high marks and teacher comments consistently confirm her diligence and talent. So when she received one of the lowest marks on her report card for participation, she was alarmed. With no mention before hand of not meeting expectations, the low mark was not only uncharacteristic of her but also a surprise to us both. Naturally, I'd have to call on the teacher for an explanation.

It's a delicate thing to advocate for your child when her grade isn't bad, but doesn't reflect her known best. So, before approaching the teacher, I asked my mom (a long time educator) about the right approach and discussed it with a friend.

I read my draft to my friend Janet. "Girlfriend, this note is much too soft; you should be more direct." I at first explained my straightforward but soft tone saying I wanted to make sure I didn't seem like one of those neurotic helicopter moms. As Janet continued to question my passivity, I fessed up to my more likely reason. The delicate dance that I—especially as a black woman— must dance to avoid being seen as aggressive, upset or angry in confrontations. Strong language, even candor can provoke this stereotype; therefore, I am cautious of my tone in written correspondence on sensitive matters. In person I am careful to ABS (Always Be Smiling) especially during conflict to allay this reaction.

"Do you really believe that?," Janet challenged. She went on to say that advocating for my daughter was important and I should feel free to be firm no matter what anyone thinks. I hung up feeling a little cowed and nettled by my fear of being seen as aggressive. Maybe Janet was right. Perhaps I was overreacting and a little paranoid in my caution.

When the teacher's response seemed casual and detached, I drafted a firmer and more detailed email outlining my concerns and issues with the grade and the response. Namely that both were unacceptable.

The teacher's reply? "Dear Mrs. Fritsch: I am sorry this grade has so upset you." And, there "it" was in the very first line. Where I was candid and firm, the teacher found me "upset" (angry). I know very well, that the teacher's concern of upset was earnest, but had a male parent drafted the same letter, the teacher may have seen logic over emotion. And while the teacher didn't directly pronounce me an 'Angry Black Woman," everything in the tone of her letter indicates she pictured me as such. This confirmed my earlier reservations-- no, fear--in being direct, serious, firm without smiley emoji and an "XOXO" valediction.

I rang Janet, "Hate to say, 'I told you so.'"

Welcome to The Angry Black Woman

I read a quote that said American women are liberated but not empowered. And, another that mentioned one's ability to have confidence, without dignity. For African-American women both liberation and dignity are ensnared in the persona of "The Angry Black Woman." Not until we can be liberated from the fear of being seen as angry in the face of serious discourse and confrontation will we be empowered to rise up and step into the fullness of our humanity. To exercise authenticity of our presence and purpose, not only have a place at the table but a voice when we get there.

You can hardly insult a black woman more than to call her "The Angry Black Woman." "The Angry Black Woman" is a stereotype most successful black women do their best to avoid, no matter that it can be nearly impossible to do so. Black women with dominant leadership traits and strong personalities are at risk even though these very same traits are success markers for white males.

Much of my own life has been built around escaping any stereotype that could in any way identify me as an 'Angry Black Woman.' The eye rolling, neck snapping, finger pointing woman who's jumping at the bit to tell off any person who works her nerves. Striving to be in control of and above this criticism, I liked to think I could direct my fate by managing myself (diction, pitch, pronounce your 'r's) and putting my best self (good manners, stand up straight and tall) and face forward (ABS: always be smiling) against the label.

Not until "The Angry Black Woman," hot potato landed on me was I astounded at my failure to recognize the full and loathsome consequences of this label. I hadn't planned to openly discuss or explore internally how being put in this category made me feel. I wasn't even aware, or, I should rather say, had not allowed myself to acknowledge just how deeply and why it burned me in my bones to be called "The Angry Black Woman."

But just like one of those moments where out of the blue, your mind goes back to an old nemesis or friend and you wonder, "What ever happened to Cheryl?," my thoughts settled on the day I was sucker punched with this label. In reflecting on my moment, these same moments endured by my single mother, and the incident with my daughter's teacher, I considered how this stereotype discourages achievement, risk-taking, inclusion, progress and gender equality in all women, black women specifically. It awakened me to the many ways this stereotype is silencing the value, experiences, and ideas of a culture, race, and gender of people under the notion that something about our anger renders us incompetent, disreputable, irrelevant, obstructive. Denying women the freedom and opportunity to unashamedly advocate for themselves and their effort. In denying us the liberty and access to an emotion that all human beings feel and experience (even Jesus got angry in the temple) we are robbed of basic humanity.

Beyond feelings of insult, I am ashamed to recognize my own bias in my determination to distance myself from being seen as "some angry black woman. A bias that does more to contribute to, rather than breakdown, the stigma and stereotype of "The Angry Black Woman." In treading so lightly in my own life, I've been overly cautious with opportunities, submissive to certain points of view, and downright neglectful of and about many of my true feelings and experiences.

Having been groomed to get ahead by working twice as hard, it's possible I've often been overly accepting and content with receiving half as much. Worse, I have erroneously viewed my presence as "the only one in the room" as proof of my own exceptionalism and esteem rather than seeing it for what it truly is: a symptom and result of something out of order and out of balance in the world. Both discourage self-expansion and advancement, but most disastrously furthers the status quo and victimizes society as a whole.

I wondered too how many other women allow this stereotype to push them into the shadows of their fullest humanity. How it has forced us still to the back of the bus and hushed our rightful place in humanity, leadership, community, acceptance. This stereotype is so lethally intimidating that it shuts us up and out before we even dare speak.

I'd been making notes in my mind about my 'Angry Black Woman' experience not knowing where it would end up. When I was invited to give a TEDx talk, I wondered if I dared speak on something so personal and volatile.

Before my TEDx, most of my speeches and public speaking appearances were political. The non-political topics I'd recently written about: audacity, judgement, brokenness, seemed unworthy of this big moment. Still, "The Angry Black Woman" seemed too out there. Daunting. Vulnerable. Daring. Would they get it? Could I present it with the dignity and integrity it deserved? More importantly, would they care and, if they did, would I do more damage than good on the subject?I'd studied and read enough on risk and authenticity to know it was precisely this risk and vulnerability that made "The Freedom To Be The Angry Black Woman," an idea worth spreading. When I shared the topic with a girlfriend (a white friend), she said, "Oh, you have to talk about that."

I hit send to the organizer and didn't breath for two days until she wrote back, "I LOVE THIS TALK." I gave God a high-five. Exhaled. This ebook is adapted from TEDx Great Hills Women in Austin, Texas. This TEDx was a sister event alongside the global TEDWomen theme, "Momentum," with the topic "The Freedom to Be."

Much to my surprise, exploring the history and magnitude of this stereotype led me to embrace rather than reject what it truly means to be "The Angry Black Woman." It gave me the freedom to accept and be "The Angry Black Woman," properly defined and understood. The TEDx was an opportunity to foster this understanding and redefine this identity.

The standing ovation this talk received along with the line of women who approached me afterwards to share examples of how they were intimidated by the notion of anger and gender and how empowered they felt hearing this talk confirmed indeed "The Freedom To Be The Angry Black Woman" is an idea worth spreading. Sharing this message from that red carpet blessed me with clarity on the mission of my life's work and purpose. And so I'm sharing it with you in writing.

My work is to continue sharing and broadening the conversation on a singular idea of our connectedness in humanity. I hope it will inspire and empower us to think different about who we are deep within ourselves and in each other and who we desire to be in the world long after we are gone.

Lisa Fritsch

The Freedom to Be "The Angry Black Woman"

I never thought this would happen to me. It's a moment I'll remember forever and a feeling I will never forget. And for the awakening of my authenticity and voice it called forth in me, I'll be eternally grateful.

My most exciting memories running for Governor of Texas happened in our war room, the strategic engine of the campaign. These sessions both exhausted and invigorated me with the realization and magnitude of our undertaking. The chutzpah, running for Governor. I couldn't allow thoughts like that to distract and overwhelm me. Our time was precious here as we vetted message, strategy, and yes, dirt. We were the underdog campaign. Underfunded and climbing uphill. Focus was key. In any campaign, in this room, strong, candid, and brutal honesty is the norm. Passions naturally run high as policies and decisions are being explored and made. Frankly there may be more ego in one room than most walls are meant to handle.

In one particularly heated session, my voice rose (excitement), I leaned in (intensity), and spoke with fervor (passion) and in a way that let others know my message had a mission. I was introducing our proposed policy on immigration, one that defied the status quo and would bring dignity and hope to immigrants. The ideas were unconventional for our state and political party so I knew I'd need a balance of emotion and logic. I was on a roll and saw that my point was building momentum. I was just at the crescendo of the most brilliant part of it all when one of my main guys said--hands up defensively, "Whoa, there. You need to calm down, Lisa. You're looking like "The Angry Black Woman." He had shut me up and down.

"Say what now, what did you say?," I heard my mind speak. I searched myself, the immediate past. Had I neck rolled? Did I curse? Were my nostrils flaring? Fist clenched? Teeth grinding? A blinding light went across my face. What just happened? I can't breathe; is it hot in here? A heatwave hit my throat, but calling on my ability (and training) to keep my cool, I feigned one of those breathy laughs, waved him off and tried to get back on topic. But after being identified as "The Angry Black Woman," the whole table turned their attention away from my point and sunk their teeth into this assessment. Seeing the confusion on my face, heated--albeit sincere--counsel rolled in about how I could under no circumstances ever be seen as "The Angry Black Woman," on the campaign trail. I would lose all credibility. The media would turn on me. The more I pushed back on the absurdity of their claims and this myth, the more the moniker stuck and the less ground I was able to gain.

And so, in order to regain ground, I was forced to back off. Having my authority compromised did in fact make me feel anger for the passion I was not permitted to show. It ended with me tight lipped, and more distraught than angry when I considered how we'd lost a chance to have a game changing discussion on immigration because my passion, not my insight became the issue. In order not to come unhinged that day, I deployed the full force of my training: ABS, shoulders back, speak in a low, calm, quiet voice, manners--Lisa, are you smiling? Ok, and yes, by then I was angry. Mad. And, though I hoped it didn't show--that my training had fooled everyone else, I was mad. Holding back tears, mad.

Why must it be always be anger and nothing else?

Where did "The Angry Black Woman" come from?

The 'Angry Black Woman' (ABW) can be traced back to the popular, The Amos n' Andy Show. Sapphire, sassy, finger-waving, neck-snapping, was the angry wife who emasculated her husband. Since that portrayal caricatures of 'The Angry Black Woman" have proliferated throughout television and media giving us "Esther" on Sanford and Son, to Tyler Perry's Madea where the moniker has crossed over as a descriptor of black women in real life.

Who Is She Really?

She is no one and yet she is too many of us. The danger is that society has widely cast any black woman who expresses strong emotion and varying degrees of humanity, exasperation in particular as "The Angry Black Woman." At some point most black women no matter their level of education, economic status, looks, or temperament will get tagged with this moniker simply in having the audacity to show up and/or expecting to be seen and heard.

This is especially true when a black woman's presence or voice defies the status quo (white privilege, white male dominance). Read: Being the only woman, or black woman in the room, arena, field, organization, etc. Women in this position risk their passion and sense of urgency being cited as anger, or irrationality when in fact their audience prematurely assumes and links anger as a natural side effect of female or black and female.

But not only do these emotions fit across gender and racial lines, but in white males these same traits are the very markers of triumph, success, creativity, and respect.

Who Gets To Be Her and Why

Intensity, passion, ambition, and anger suit white males, who get to be every bit of "The Angry Black Woman" to their advantage. Several leaders we know and respect for their success embody many traits assigned to the 'Angry Black Woman.' They too are the 'Angry Black Woman,' and it's a high privilege.

Donald Trump

My personal favorite of this in a reverse gender example is Donald Trump. Trump pulls off ABW better than anyone I've ever seen and it hasn't hurt his success one bit.

From hair woes to the pooched out lip when he's unimpressed, to the excessive shoulder and hand gestures, and the finger pointed, "You're fired," Trump gets to be ABW without being labeled as angry. Instead he is a resilient go-getter, a fighter. A winner!

Steve Jobs

It was written that Steve Jobs responded to an eager college student, "Leave us alone," when she persisted for an interview. I don't know too many women, black or white who would go there even when they wanted to for fear that they'd be labeled as "angry," or another unkind word that rhymes with stitch.

Jobs, known for his explosive personality, is not characterized as angry. In fact many have linked his anger and passion to his drive and creativity. No one has ever considered that his anger diminished his genius. Rather they surmise, it likely enhanced it.

When is the last time you've seen an assertive, passionate white man in a leadership role be labeled as angry? Eccentric. Maybe rude, but never angry.

Well, okay there are exceptions. Bravo to a few men whose pictures game up in a Google image search for "The Angry Black Woman." Newt Gingrich, Ted Turner, and Fifty Cent. (Way to represent Fiddy.)

Who Doesn't Get to Be Her and Why Not

If you are a woman or a black woman especially, you are not permitted to wear this label with dignity, respect or grace. In fact, nothing scares a successful black woman more than being called, "The Angry Black Woman." Following are some notable and modern examples across several platforms where this stereotype is aptly and often applied with derogatory means and measure.

Michelle Obama

Sadly, one of the first issues our First Lady Michelle Obama had to address was to defend herself against this stereotype. Educated, successful, assertive and passionate about her views for education and working class Americans she declared publicly and very early on, "I'm not some 'Angry Black Woman.'"

First Lady Obama delivered a powerful speech on her experiences growing up black in America to graduates at Tuskegee University. She openly discussed the frustrations of being draped in negative stereotypes and the unique pressures she faced as the first African-American First Lady. She revealed the vulnerability she felt when her first magazine cover, The New Yorker, cartooned her in an afro with a machine gun and tagged the innocent fist bump with President Obama, then Presidential nominee, as a "terrorist fist jab." She opened up about the fine line any black woman in the limelight walks between respect and ridicule.

Nearly all but those who share her experience saw her speech as "bitter," "divisive," "angry."

Shonda Rhimes

Though roles and characters of black women and women have evolved, Amos n' Andy's Sapphire of more than 60 years ago remains with us. This ugly version of the stereotype continues to make its way to the center of entertainment's most creative and successful artists despite their unique talent and contributions to their field.

Shonda Rhimes, a brilliant writer and storyteller with the some of the biggest hits in television history such as Grey's Anatomy, Scandal, and How to Get Away With Murder, was hit with "The Angry Black Woman" label after a columnist decided Rimes' leading women--many of whom are black--were "molded in her image" as "The Angry Black Woman." These characters, the actresses, and Ms. Rimes herself are highly educated, powerful, and determined women earning success in a male dominated arena. There must be other ways to define them without using "The Angry Black Woman," which threatens to overshadow and undermine the milestones they've made in their fields. No doubt anger had a lot less to do with her success than perseverance, talent, determination, and craft.

Rhimes was incensed and rightly so. She responded indignantly to the idea that she and her characters were whittled down to an updated version of Sapphire. Sixty years of progress removed with a few strokes of a pen. With those four words the New York Times writer's piece sought to undermine and discredit many years of effort, progress and the inherent genius at the core of Ms. Rhimes' narrative.

Serena Williams

In tennis--and many would argue any other sport--there is no one more dominant in the game, than Serena Williams. Before focusing on Serena herself, it's important to sit a bit longer with the fact that Serena's sport is tennis.

In sports dominance, aggression, ambition, and fight even among women (volleyball, soccer, basketball) wouldn't be extraordinary to mention. But tennis is a gentrified and expensive sport long dominated by white men and women of privilege and pedigree. It's also a sport, like golf, that until recently was largely absent champions of color. And, like golf, tennis is often described as a "thinking" or strategic game over one that can be conquered by sheer physical will and prowess.

Before Serena and her sister Venus, African-American tennis players of status and notoriety, Arthur Ashe, Althea Gibson, Zena Garrison, were gentle and benign. They won but they didn't dominate. And, while they certainly broke down barriers and stereotypes in the game, they simply weren't a threat to the tennis status quo.

Serena and her sister came onto the tennis court like a hurricane. Everything about them was a loud and overriding disruption. From their story, their dark skin, their braided hair with beads (a purposeful move says their mother Oracene so that they would be affirmed in who they were), and their game, unapologetically defied the tennis establishment.

At first the establishment and their opponents hoped their lack of establishment preparation would render their power game one-dimensional and unsustainable. They'd hoped Martina Hingis, "a smart player," would be a deterrent. She was not. The media speculated that the sisters might be unable to handle the pressure and the off-court volleying required of the sport's top athletes. They conquered tennis while pursuing fashion, expanded their education, wrote books and even played less tennis and extended their career so far into their mid-thirties. Commentators and media were quick to observe and admire their "athleticism" rather than acknowledge their prudence and constitution off the court.

Serena began to stand out. While Venus played a powerful game, she played with steely calm and reserve. Staring only into her strings, walking quietly on changeovers, barely raising a fist on her most victorious points. Serena played with an in your face fire that said, "your butt is mine." Winners and questionable calls were met with a stare down. Victorious points were followed by a thundering, "Come on!!," complete with a raised racket and veins in the neck.

It's no surprise then that Serena--more than Venus-- would fall victim to the ABW stereotype. For more than fourteen years both sisters refused to to play tennis at Indian Wells due to a racial incident. But it was a 2012 US Open final where Serena was called for a foot fault during a very intense match that kept people talking for too long. Serena did in fact get angry. She had choice words for the umpire, all the while waving her racket like a weapon. She was "The Angry Black Woman."

But so too was John McEnroe. Marat Safin. Even Roger Federer has become angry on the court in nearly the same if not in more egregious ways. "Meh" we say. The list is long of men in other sports who get away with the passion, heat, and the intensity of the moment during a game--who after it is all over are free to move on without a relentless accountability for a heated moment on the court or field. We expect and revel in their intensity. We don't indict their character. We apply the full content of who they are and what they bring to the game.

Finally, it wasn't just the Williams' talent. What really seemed to irk and displease the critics were that they couldn't be sufficiently humbled--not by losses, by awe of an opponent, by the game, by racism, by the privilege of others. The sisters were audacious, bold, daring, and unapologetic about who they were. Their father was vocal and critical of media and the tennis establishment about the impact of race in the sport. Many thought Richard Williams was paranoid about race and tennis, race in America. He was seen as arrogant (he had no money yet, proclaimed to the tennis elite that he had, not one but, two daughters who would take the game by storm and be #1 and #2 in the world. This (before it came to pass) had many people laughing at his delusions of grandeur. On top of it all the girls were not bashful or modest about winning and their desire to win and be the best. They expected to win and they did.

Sports writer and tennis commentator, Jon Wertheim said it best, "The Williams sisters wield authority like no other players. Were they male, we would applaud their 'intensity' their 'competitive streak' their 'ferocity.' Because they are women—black women, no less—they are 'catty,' and 'lack humility'."

Why it's Dangerous

"The Angry Black Woman" follows us at home and in our communities as well. When I told a friend about this talk, she shared with me how this happens frequently in her home when she and her husband are having an argument. "Often my husband will dismiss me as being angry in our arguments rather than try to understand why I might be angry in the first place."

And, this is a greater point often overlooked. Might some of these women, might I, have a reason to be angry? Might others who are quick to make accusations of anger do so out of subconscious knowing that there's something for these women to be angry about? That were they in the same position, they too would be angry? And so in order to be disconnected from the other person's experience or the responsibility to change, accusing the person of anger becomes a tool to box them in and put them in their place. Settling the matter once and for all that the status quo is entitled to its position and should therefore remain.

But it isn't as basic and simple as anger. What people misidentify as anger is passion and a sense of urgency to gain for ourselves in the world what has so long been denied: love, acceptance, purpose. Yes, anger may play a role in our intensity and boldness and our desire, but where anger may be the catalyst, love is the reason.

Dominant and determined black women are not angry. We're intense because there's a lot at stake. We are not angry, but sensitive because we care so deeply. We are not bitter about our position or ungrateful for how far we have come. We are passionate because there's much more to be done. And, we are not upset about the uphill climb, but we have arrived with fire and grit because it hasn't been easy. So forgive us if you find the sweat on our brows, the intensity of our gestures, and the heaviness of heart lacking in grace and pretense. This journey has made us real with a low tolerance for bull.

Dominant and determined black women are not angry, we are under immense pressure. Pressure to measure up to the highest ideal in manner, fashion, aptitude, appearance, communication, decorum, speech, style. The pressure to be wise and prudent in hair choice so often misjudged as a statement of politics, social and economic standing. Finally, there's the oppression of all that a potential failure means. The pressure that failure reflects poorly not only on oneself but is a shame and detriment to all of your gender and race. ("Poise." "Be excellent." And then more directly, plainly, in case the former directives were too vague, "Don't do anything to make us look bad," my grandmother reminded every time I went where I was sure to be one of few black young women in the room, my training in full force.) A shame with expansive and enduring consequences, endangering opportunities of those of your gender and race who come with or after you.

Dominant and determined black women are not angry; we are frustrated. With this pressure comes a supernatural pressure to be seen as invincible and be invulnerable to most human expression: sadness, explosive glee, disappointment, confusion, weakness, uncertainty. Many displays of emotion are intolerable for they can be misread and mislead the status quo into thinking you cannot measure up. Weaknesses. Out of the question. Uncertainty. Never. Strong emotions (except for expressed pleasure at your arrival and for those joining you at the table) signal incompetence, or even worse, an inability to handle the pressure--the pressure that the status quo (white men) are equipped and bred to conquer. Thus, you are permitted to be seen as the 'Strong Black Woman' (though this comes with its own set of neurosis and fated disasters as well) so long as you are never the 'Angry Black Woman.'

Not only must we willingly climb uphill (work twice as hard), but we must "always be smiling," steady as we go, so that it looks effortless to boot. Otherwise, someone might get the idea that you're offended or angry, which automatically disqualifies you from being worthy of your destination at the top.

The result with every advancing step--pressure mounting, history at stake, and personal accountability on the line--is a lingering and festering paranoia that others (the status quo) hope you fail. That you will be put in your rightful place. Below, beneath, under, a little lower now. Perhaps seen but certainly unheard. And, you can fail in different, same ways. You can fail outright by losing, in not being the best, or by losing your temper. All proving in equal measure what the world believes in the first place, you aren't good enough.

That your (mine, ours, women, black women's) success exposes the illegitimacy of the status quo's presumed superiority increases the intensity, the sense of urgency, and the passion. The idea that our success is a threat to the way things have always been done means the interest of the establishment to protect the status quo is as strong as our desire to break it down. And so forgive us, if at our arrival you find us sometimes stoic, withdrawn, and aloof in manner. Many of us are trying our best to be strong, but not angry. We are looking for the balance of cheerfulness (ABS) minus explosive (loud) jubilation. In short, we are trying to mimic you while navigating a way to lend the very essence and core of ourselves that we'd not like to lose. Forgive us if sometimes in doing so we become more like you than you'd like, determined, pushy, bossy and yes, a little entitled too. All in all, given the opportunity, our presence and voice can serve both our interests of living in a better world.

This label stigmatizes us and victimizes society at large. We relegate to the shadows a force of women who could be flourishing and succeeding if given the liberty and opportunity to do so. Academy Award winner Viola Davis said, "The only thing that separates women of color from anyone else is opportunity." I believe this stereotype goes a long way in denying those opportunities. Here's how.

Silencing an Experience

Mrs. Obama's openness about her experiences makes certain people uncomfortable. Critics see Rhimes' work as driven by anger, rather than her gift and dedication to her craft. Serena's detractors overlook her successes and humanity off the court and her drive to be the best competitor she can be. How is it that merely being angry or showing anger can overshadow all other narratives of one's experience? And, is there a legitimate reason for these women to be angry that makes critics eagerly grab onto anger in defining their passion and identities?

When we're anxious that we play a role in a negative experience, taking the shortcut to anger blaming lets us off the hook. We can easily discredit someone with a point and experience contrary to ours by judging their point of view irrational and therefore irrelevant. By dismissing their experience in this way, we are relieved from expressing empathy or understanding. Further, we have no need to question our fears, motives and presuppositions. Essentially this invalidates the whole person. But if we don't have to listen, dig deeper, think different, grow, and challenge what we believe, we hurt ourselves and stunt our own humanity. Our refusal to listen allows us to invalidate not only the heart of their message, but also who they are, and who we could become.

The tables turn when our audience empathizes or shares our experience. They are more likely to see passion for what it truly is and to recognize the true intention of our actions and words--love, acceptance, purpose. Flip the audience to those who don't share the experience or relate to our story, and the assessment can become anger, bitterness. This prevails in all instances from the First Lady to my friend.

In the case of our First Lady, her critics immediately pushed back that her speech was trite, negative, and well… angry. Critics even blasted her for "playing the race card." Where critics saw anger, the students in her audience saw humility and truth. They appreciated her candor for the similarity to their own experiences growing up black in America. They didn't see her as angry, rather motivational and courageous.

While to the New York Times critic, Ms. Rhimes and her characters call to mind angry black women, fans of Ms. Rhimes, her shows, and her characters, see these women as powerful voices and examples of their potential a long time coming. They are proud of these characters and the portrayal of strength, dominance and success they reveal to the world about women and the multi-faceted dimensions in us all.

Serena's fans understand her intensity and find it inspirational rather than unsportsmanlike. Serena's fans know her intense "Come ons!!" are the lifted voice of a champion who, against all earthly odds, dominates an arena where a voice and game like hers was nonexistent before her.

Where critics in all these circumstances see an angry woman, fans and supporters find hope and validation. They see someone who has earned the right to their leadership, audacity, and authenticity the hard way. Until we make a distinction between anger and assertiveness—anger and passion—anger and audacity—anger and dominance, our world will suffer the consequences of the silencing and the demise of a people.

In "We Should All Be Feminists," a book based on her TedTalk, Chimamanda Ngozi Adichie addresses the importance of breaking down and accepting our experiences.

"I was once talking about gender and a man said to me, 'Why does it have to be you as a woman? Why not you as a human being?' This type of question is a way of silencing a person's specific experiences. Of course I am a human being, but there are particular things that happen to me in the world because I am a woman."

The same example applies to black women on an even more profound level. I was often asked during my political tenure, why the need to label something as a "black experience," or why'd I have to say, "As an African-American woman?"

It's okay to see my color just as it is okay to see that I am tall. I am happy being me, female me, black me. It's disingenuous and perilous to see me but subtract my legacy, heritage, and the experiences I've had as me--this includes being black and female as well as East Texan and tall. Eagerly trying to remove all traces of race and color in hopes that we can live peacefully in a healed world without prejudices, does more to advance racial and social injustice by silencing the voice of a specific experience. Rather than giving significance to the underrepresented, people who think this way, are advocating a further removal of representation of the underrepresented and the impact of their voice. Prejudices break down when we can openly discuss our experiences free from judgment and annoyance. Not when we silence them all together, or pretend they are all the same.

Silencing a Group of Women

It's interesting how we marvel and often raise up and admire the successful black men who attribute their success to being raised by a single black woman without considering the management, leadership, and skills in diplomacy she must have had to make this possible all on her own. Without considering all the things that must have indeed made her angry enough to do better for herself and her family. Where anger may have been the catalyst, love was the reason.

Our world is missing out on the wealth of knowledge and experience of black women. Women who are brimming with passion and creativity. Women who know how to stretch a dollar. Women who know how to market and talk to other women. Women who understand what it is like to hold one's head up high even when the soul is downcast. These are all leadership strengths in humility and logic that are valuable to business and society.

Many women remain silent because they do not have the freedom to be unapologetically passionate. They know the thin line they walk in business and culture between being seen as loud and brash versus assertive and capable. Mislabeling passion as anger, organizations suffer the void of good ideas and new ways to solve problems because they shut down rather than listen up. Women and black women especially remain silent across several industries: tech, finance, elected government and leadership, and oil and gas — the list goes on— not only because they don't speak up but because they aren't even there to do so in the first place.

"The Angry Black Woman" stereotype creates barriers and biases that bar many doors to progress, social uplift, and economic advancement.

Black women make up only 3 percent of board seats at Fortune 500 companies. As I write this, Ursula Burns is the lone black female chief executive in all of Fortune 500 companies. And, Burns who describes herself as having a "big mouth," with "patience not being one of my strengths," is no wall flower. Nor can she be to effectively do her job.

According to a study by Northwestern University's Kellogg School of Management, "Black women were evaluated comparable to white male leaders who displayed dominant and assertive behavior."

Further existing studies have shown that, "professional white men have been granted greater status and power when they've expressed anger rather than sadness."

Black women must be empowered to have passion, pluck, candor and raise the stakes and their voices same as the likes of Donald Trump and Steve Jobs without people assuming they've lowered their IQ and the ability to be logical.

Reclaiming Our Humanity

I want the freedom to be "The Angry Black Woman." I crave the freedom to passionately defend strong positions, present strong ideas, and defy the status quo without the intimidation of being mislabeled and misjudged. I and other women want to be seen through the full comprehension of our character, actions, and experiences. I believe every human being deserves that.

Originally when I wrote this for my TEDx, I thought I would talk on how we should change the 'A' to less threatening adjectives—those we can all rally behind, that don't make us uncomfortable: "The Audacious, Ambitious, or, The Assertive Black Woman."

But that sets the bar too low. This bypasses connectedness for conformity. The whole point in our human connectedness is to understand and accept that to be human employs an array of emotions.

We can do better than to relabel a stereotype.

It's so much better to recognize how we're all "The Angry Black Woman" (or have been) at some point in our lives—no matter our ethnicity or gender. Haven't we all had an instance where we've gotten fired up, loud, and emotive, eager to have others share our sense of urgency.

The goal for unity and peace is for us to see ourselves in one another. This includes seeing ourselves in one another's stereotypes. I am at times "the valley girl" who freaks out near spiders, or, my "redneck" East Texas self preferring "Boot Scoot Boogie" to Bach and Chopin. We are all a sum and a continuum of one another. We must resist the urge to deny certain people the freedom, because of their race, ethnicity, or gender, to exhibit all forms of humanity. To hold a certain group of us to a standard of perfection that we fail to meet ourselves. In the words of Rumi, "We are all here to walk each other home."

Besides this, the idea isn't to redefine the proper way for black women or any woman to conform in order to be taken seriously, or to be seen as a human being. We must educate ourselves to the value women with these traits bring us and to think differently about the role anger can play in gender. What we want is to be able to relate to and understand one another. And to think different about our perceptions of anger and women.

First, anger is a part of being human. We are programmed to get angry and there are varying degrees of anger. Anger doesn't always mean wrath and vein popping vengefulness.

Like happiness, sadness, and wonder, anger is a human emotion like an array of others that isn't constant but can also be useful in the right context.

Finally, anger has it's upsides. Christy Matta, a behavioral therapist and researcher tells us that anger can serve an important purpose. Anger helps us overcome difficult obstacles, right wrongs, stand up for ourselves and others. Anger alerts us to those things that are important to us. And, get this, it is possible to be angry and stay in control of how you behave. According to The Scientific Monitor research has shown that anger can lead to creative flow and thinking outside the box. i.e.: Steve Jobs.

Here is the what one really needs to know about "The Angry Black Woman" and who she truly is.

1. She's awesome—Usually, ABW has had to overcome several obstacles in life towards present opportunities. This uphill climb can fuel to her resolve and dedication.
2. She's dedicated—She sees a need in causes where others don't and makes a difference in our world.
3. She's authentic—She will tell you the truth and the world can benefit from her experiences, insight, and versatile wisdom. Yes, there may be a neck roll, but a neck roll has never hurt anyone.
4. She's a doer—She's a mover and shaker not content with the status quo.
5. She's fierce-- She's afraid but does it anyway.

"The Angry Black Woman" is essential to us as we speak up and out, break down barriers, and push forward. "The Angry Black Woman" is sensitive because she cares so deeply. She's passionate because there is a lot at stake and a lot more work to get done.

Think where we would be in our society today without all "The Angry Black Women" who put progress over posture. Think of the women who have gone before us who saw a situation that made them angry and took a passionate and unwavering stand to create a better world. For where anger may have been the catalyst, love was the reason. When I'm tempted to back down, speak more softly, or to just grin and bear it, I think of them, and I give myself permission to rise. Thank you Harriet Tubman, Rosa Parks, Michelle Obama, Shonda Rhimes, Condoleeza Rice, Maya Angelou, Toni Morrison, Sojourner Truth, mother, my grandmothers, my great-grandmothers, and any woman who dares live a dream that will outlive her life. OPRAH. These are our sisters, our legacy, our legitimacy and our permission to be.

I want the freedom to be just like them, all of them. I want Elenor to be empowered to put progress over posture. For her to not only have confidence, but dignity. That she not only be liberated, but empowered. I will not teach her to work twice as hard and settle for half as much. I will teach her to rise in passion and truth and to use her voice boldly and often. I will teach her to revere this notion of "The Angry Black Woman." Because I see now when I was called, "The Angry Black Woman," I shouldn't have been insulted. I should have been proud. Because where anger may have been the catalyst, love was the reason.

Other Titles By Lisa Fritsch:

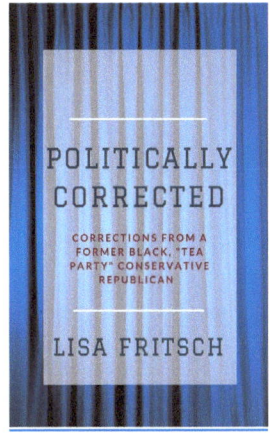

Obama, Tea Parties and GOD   Politically Corrected

After spending fifteen years as a dedicated conservative activist with a wide ranging platform in print talk radio, television, consulting and speaking, Lisa Fritsch answered a calling to make a run for Governor of Texas in the Republican Primary. Fritsch was led to bring a new voice to conservative values that included giving voice to the underrepresented. Yet, it was on this journey that God corrected and humbled both her politics and her heart. "What God revealed to me on the trail in my suffering, the suffering of those I met, and in my arrogance of "knowing best," transformed and renewed my mind. In moving from politics to people, I'm sharing with you the corrections that called me away from the 'black, conservative, Tea Party, Republican' road to humility and love. I hope these corrections will also touch your spirit and call you to care less about how people vote and much more you love them."

About Lisa Fritsch

Lisa Fritsch is a social and political strategist and advocate for the underrepresented. She's been a social and political activist for nearly 15 years. Lisa was a talk-radio show host for over 12 years and a national radio and television commentator appearing regularly on Fox News Channel's "Glenn Beck," "Your World with Neil Cavuto," and Fox News 7. She has also appeared on MSNBC, CNN, BET, and Univision and has been featured and/or published in internet publications and newspapers such as The Huffington Post, The Daily Beast, Breitbart, The Blaze, The Dallas Morning News, The Washington Times, The Austin American Statesman, World Net Daily and many more.

Lisa ran in the 2014 Republican Primary for Governor of Texas to challenge the status quo and an agenda to represent the underrepresented: women's rights, dignity for immigrants, education reform, entrepreneurial access and opportunity for all Texans including the 18% of working Texans living in poverty, her campaign raised consciousness across Texas and nationwide receiving endorsements from BAMPAC, Central Texas Coalition for Life, National Republican Trust PAC and Texans United for Reform and Freedom.

Lisa is the Executive Director of the PHENOMENALISM.org (launching in 2016 with phenomenal stories), a non-profit equipping women of color to lead globally in the 21st century and creator of The Humility Project, a research and story sharing blog navigating humility as the path to peace, power, and purpose.

EXPANDING
LOVE·CONSCIOUSNESS·PURPOSE

www.lisafritsch.com

www.thehumilityproject.org

www.phenomenalism.org

www.ingramcontent.com/pod-product-compliance
Lightning Source LLC
Chambersburg PA
CBHW050909290526
45792CB00002B/751